# ADELITA
## A Sea Turtle's Journey

Jenny Goebel

illustrated by Ana Miminoshvili

Albert Whitman & Company
Chicago, Illinois

Under a moonlit sky, and below rough, coarse sand, a loggerhead sea turtle was born. She emerged from a squishy egg buried deep in the ground.

When the time came, she rose and rose and rose, among a boil of other hatchlings.

She was the size of a silver dollar. Her shell was soft and new. Her head bobbed. Her flippers fluttered. She skittered across the beach.

*Snap.* She narrowly escaped a seabird's pointy beak.

*Click.* She dodged the sharp pincers of a crab. Guided by the light of the moon, she slipped into the lapping ocean waves.

She propelled herself forward. Beating her flippers rapidly, she swam until she found cover in dense seaweed. There, she hid from sharks and whales and long-nosed barracuda.

When she was tired, she drifted on swift-moving currents and was carried deeper and deeper into the ocean.

The larger and hungrier she grew, the farther she wandered from home.
She wandered.
And wandered.
She wandered until she found a place to feast on lobsters and red crabs.
She wandered until a fisherman found her.

By then, she had grown to roughly the size of a dinner plate.

"You are not safe in the Gulf of California, my friend," the fisherman said. "Hunters are trapping sea turtles for food. They're selling their shells to be turned into decorations."

The fisherman brought the young sea turtle
to a group of researchers studying marine life in
Baja California, Mexico. The researchers fed the
loggerhead, bathed her, and watched over her.
She stared back at them with big, black eyes.

Years went by. The sea turtle grew and grew and grew, until she was large-headed, strong-jawed, and as wide as a manhole cover.

She lingered near one side of her cramped tank. The side closest to the ocean.

A young researcher named Wallace Nichols watched over her with extra care. "Where is your home?" he asked. "How far did you swim to get here?"

There wasn't a single nesting beach anywhere near Baja, and yet there were many loggerheads all along the coastline. Wallace and his team thought they might know where the turtles were coming from, but it seemed too far away. What if they could find out if sea turtles were capable of swimming great distances?

Wallace knew a way.

Researchers were just starting to use satellite transmitters to track marine life, and Wallace had a used satellite tag. The research team could return their sea turtle to the ocean and use the tag to gather information as she swam.

Finally, they could try to solve the mystery of where all the loggerheads in Baja were coming from.

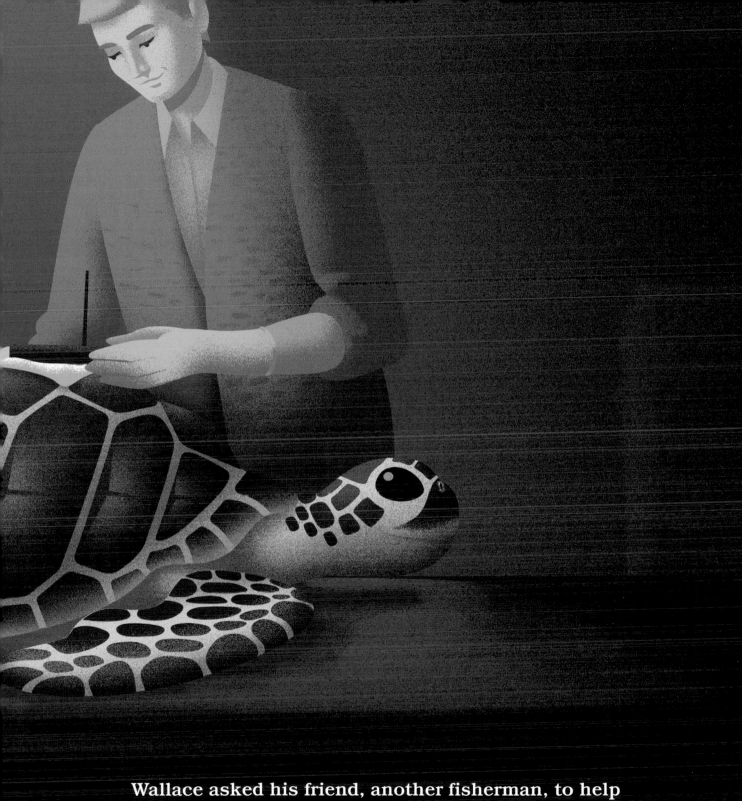

Wallace asked his friend, another fisherman, to help him attach the satellite tag to the loggerhead's shell with a strong but harmless glue.

"I'm going to call you Adelita," the fisherman said. "The same name I gave my daughter."

Wallace and the fisherman took Adelita out in a small boat called a panga. They circled the waves until they found the perfect spot. They lifted Adelita over the side. They gently let her go.

Wallace was happy and sad all at once. He was excited to set Adelita free, but he was also worried. The loggerhead was healthy, but was she fit enough to survive her journey?

Adelita held back at first. Perhaps she was also happy and sad. Perhaps she was worried too. But there were no longer walls to stop her. She swam away.

While she swam, the satellite tag attached to her shell transmitted her location. Using this data, Wallace created a website to map her progress.

Before long, her story caught the attention
of more than just researchers and scientists.
Schoolchildren and turtle lovers also took interest.
Soon, millions of people from all over the planet
were tracking Adelita's journey on their computers.

What a journey it was!
Adelita swam and swam and swam.
She swam past rugged Guadalupe Island.
She rose above the waves to breathe in salty sea air.
She rested in caves.

The ocean was a dangerous place—full of trash, hooks, nets, and barren stretches. Not to mention hungry, wide-eyed predators.

But Adelita was bolder now. Her shell was harder, and she was much larger and stronger than the last time she'd made this journey.

She swam past the volcanic islands of Hawaii.

She swam past sharks and whales and long-nosed barracuda.

She swam past the ring-shaped French Frigate Shoals. Past remote Wake Island. She was determined to reach the sandy shore where she was born. It was calling her home. Watchers from around the world wondered, "Will Adelita ever stop swimming?"

No—not for over a year, at least. Adelita swam for 368 long days.

Everyone was amazed as she swam thousands and thousands of miles, all the way to—

Japan!
Adelita swam across an entire ocean basin. How far she traveled was astounding. She'd spent most of her life in a tank, yet she knew exactly where to go once she was free.

Mexico

After an incredible journey, she finally reached the same waters she'd slipped into the night she was born. Adelita's voyage was complete, and Wallace and his team had their answer. Adelita, and loggerheads like her, swam unbelievable distances to return home in order to mate and lay eggs.

Japan

But there was another lesson to be learned from Adelita's journey.

Shortly after she arrived in the coastal waters of Japan, her transmitter went silent. No one knows for certain why her transmitter stopped working. It was common, however, for sea turtles to be caught in nets while swimming in fishing ports.

Those nets were keeping turtles from reaching shorelines and building new nests, and they may have stopped Adelita too.

Now that the fishermen knew the turtles had come such a long way, they began releasing them from their nets.

Just as the fishermen wanted to do better,
so did others. Children raised funds to study
additional sea turtle voyages. Researchers looked
for new ways to protect the turtles as they swam.

Adelita's journey drew people from all over the
planet closer together. She touched hearts and
inspired change—change that made our oceans a
little bit safer for other sea turtles.

Today, more loggerheads are able to complete their own incredible journeys and return to the beaches where they were born.
Adelita made a difference.

# Author's Note

The complete story of Adelita's life is impossible to know. But some facts are clear: Adelita was a loggerhead sea turtle accidentally netted by a fisherman near Baja California, Mexico, in 1986. She was held in captivity by Mexican researchers for more than a decade. A graduate student named Wallace J. Nichols first encountered and began caring for Adelita in 1992. In August of 1996, while working with other researchers and a marine biologist from Mexico's Centro Regional de Investigación Pesquera, Nichols oversaw the attachment of a satellite tag to Adelita's shell. He then set her free in the Pacific Ocean, just off the coast of Santa Rosaliíta.

Nichols shared information about Adelita's journey online and answered questions emailed from around the world. Not only was Adelita the first sea turtle tracked across an ocean basin, but thanks to the internet (which was new at that time), millions of kids were able to trace her route alongside Nichols and his team. They drew pictures, wrote poems, and cheered for her as she voyaged across the Pacific.

Traveling at a pace of approximately twenty miles a day, Adelita continuously swam west and slightly north for a year and three days. She swam more than seven thousand miles!

Adelita helped confirm what scientists speculated, that loggerhead turtles return to the same beaches where they were born in order to lay their eggs. Everyone hoped Adelita would make her own nest on a beach in Japan—something scientists believe was the purpose of her journey.

Sadly, it's unlikely she succeeded. Adelita's satellite tag stopped transmitting shortly after she arrived in the waters off Japan. She was last recorded in a fishing port along the coast. Nichols later visited the port but was unable to discover her fate. However, he did learn that a number of loggerheads were netted that summer. It is assumed Adelita was among them.

Nearly all species of sea turtles are classified as endangered. Beyond natural threats, thousands die every year when caught in nets or snagged on hooks baited for fish. Even more die due to plastic debris in the ocean and other hazards caused by humans.

Still, as is so often the case, some good came from tragedy.

Adelita really did touch hearts. She drew people across the world closer together. They felt her loss and were inspired to make changes. Fishermen took a greater interest in sea turtles. Many started cutting them free from their nets. Scientists realized that if loggerheads like Adelita were traveling such immense distances, conservation efforts had to expand. Children raised funds to study other sea turtle migrations. Wallace J. Nichols has devoted his career to protecting the ocean and its marine life.

Adelita was the first sea turtle tracked across an ocean basin, but countless others make their own incredible journeys every year. Many are now being tracked the same way Adelita was—with satellite tags attached to their shells. With each turtle's journey, we learn a little more about the big, blue ocean. We learn how everything is connected: the turtles to other marine life, the marine life to the ocean, the ocean to us, and us to one another.

The ocean is safer for sea turtles today than when Adelita raced across the Pacific. But only by a little. There is still much to do. If sea turtles are to survive, we must never forget what Adelita taught us—that people all over the planet must work together to provide safe passage for our great wanderers of the sea.

## Time Line

**1957**  Sputnik, the world's first satellite, is launched into space.

**1960s**  Scientists use radio transmitters to track wildlife.

**1978**  Loggerhead sea turtles are listed as threatened under the Endangered Species Act.

**1986**  Adelita is accidentally netted by a fisherman in the Gulf of California.

**1990s**  Advances in technology make it possible for marine animals to be tracked by satellite.

**1991**  The World Wide Web opens to the public.

**1995**  Use of the internet expands to a much broader audience with the launch of Internet Explorer, Amazon, Yahoo, and eBay. Java, a programming language for websites, is created.

**1996**  On August 10, Adelita is released in the Pacific Ocean near Santa Rosalííta, Mexico.

**1997**  On August 13, Adelita is last recorded near a fishing port off the coast of Japan.

**2010s**  Thanks to conservation efforts, the world's population of loggerhead sea turtles slowly begins to rebound.

## Online Resources

**To learn more about Adelita's journey**

The original web page for the tracking project: http://www.turtles.org/adelita.htm

Wallace J. Nichols writes about Adelita on his website: http://www.wallacejnichols.org/234/142/oceans-adelita-heart-of-a-revolution.html

Interview with Wallace J. Nichols: https://www.pbs.org/wnet/nature/voyage-of-the-lonely-turtle-interview-wallace-j-nichols/2508/

## Additional Links

Sea Turtle Conservancy: https://conserveturtles.org/

Oceanic Society: https://www.oceanicsociety.org/projects/sea-turtle-conservation

Satellite Tracking: http://www.seaturtle.org/tracking/

**For my ocean-loving in-laws,
Phil, Jane, Tim, and Kailey—JG**

**For my parents—AM**

Library of Congress Cataloging-in-Publication data
is on file with the publisher.
Text copyright © 2020 by Jenny Goebel
Illustrations copyright © 2020 by Albert Whitman & Company
Illustrations by Ana Miminoshvili
First published in the United States of America in 2020
by Albert Whitman & Company
ISBN 978-0-8075-8114-8 (hardcover)
ISBN 978-0-8075-8115-5 (ebook)
Printed in China
10  9  8  7  6  5  4  3  2  1  RRD  24  23  22  21  20

Design by Rick DeMonico

For more information about Albert Whitman & Company,
visit our website at www.albertwhitman.com.